50 Awesome Things To Do In Retirement

Berger McDonald

ISBN-13: 978-1976144707
ISBN-10: 1976144701

First Edition: September 2017
10 9 8 7 6 5 4 3 2 1

CONTENTS

Introduction

Congratulations on reaching that point in life where you can sit back, put your feet up and enjoy retirement.

Just think of it, no more cares, no more hurry and... no more paychecks! Yikes!

The first day of retirement is an exciting time. You get to sleep in until noon, then sit around in your pajamas all day.

There are lots of soap operas to catch up on and then of course all those small jobs around the house you've been putting off for years.

That was always the plan, right?

But the reality is you'll still get up at 7 a.m. every morning, looking in the mirror and wonder what to do with yourself.

Maybe you'll head out to Starbucks and nurse a coffee all day.

Or you could just sit on the porch and scratch yourself as people go by.

Those options don't appeal to you? Well then, you've discovered the ultimate book on retirement just in time.

Welcome to retirement!

You've had a long fulfilling life so far but you're not ready to be put out to pasture yet, are you?

You just need some ideas of what to do with yourself... and you'll find them here.

In this book you will discover the best things you absolutely must do to enjoy your retirement to the fullest such as:

- Joining a Nudist Club... It's a jiggle fest and a giggle fest

- Dancing... Men will hate it, women will love it

- Get a Sex Change... for guys that had man boobs anyway

- The Art and Science of Napping... and yes there is

- Smoke Pot... Join the movement, it's a joint effort

- Check out Cemeteries... Your last rodeo

- Gamble in Vegas Baby! What happens there stays there

And so much, much more...

Some of you will have a full list of things you've always wanted to do once you had the time, and others may be scratching their heads and over one important question.

Now What?

This book is written for everyone entering retirement, but especially for those in the **'now what'** dilemma.

Chapter 1: Join The Fun Activities

(1) B o w l i n g   L e a g u e

WHERE ELSE CAN YOU SIT AROUND, DRINK BEER, GET UP AND BOWL FOR 5 SECONDS THEN SIT DOWN AND DRINK BEER AGAIN?

Bowling used to be a big deal back in the 50's and 60's. Then it pretty much became something you took your kids to for birthday parties. Well, it's back again and it's the perfect sport for seniors.

Did I say sport? Well, what I meant to say was sport-ish. Yes! That's it. Think about it. There's drinking involved and athletes do that, and there's scoring and all sports keep score, right?

Umm, okay, I guess that's where the similarities end, but it's a lot of fun.

You don't have to be good, and you can even ask the alley manager to put up the bumpers. That's a little railing that rises up and blocks the gutters. It's what they use for small kids to keep the balls out of the gutter and in the alley.

The best part of the whole thing is that you get to wear funny shoes. They call them bowling shoes, but I think they're really just rejects from clown school.

The really good bowlers have their own shoes, but you'll want to rent yours, at least until you're sure this is a pastime you can handle.

You could even join a league and meet new people. Then go out together afterwards and talk about that split you missed in the second frame or the spare you picked up in the 5th. Sort of like golf but with bigger balls.

(2) Nudist Resort

A PLACE TO JUST HANG OUT AND BE SEEN.

Okay, so this one takes a little guts. You should probably practice being a nudist at home first before going to a real resort.

Start by taking off your clothes and standing in front of a full-length mirror.

Next, maintain eye contact with your reflection in the mirror and start talking. If you look down and start giggling, start over. Once you've mastered the art of straight-faced conversation with yourself in the mirror, you're ready for the real thing.

Find a resort and get yourself a day pass. You don't want to over commit with a full membership just in case this turns out not to be your thing.

Find the pool or the beach, that's where everyone will be hanging out. Observe from a distance at first and identify the alpha male. Be sure to avoid him. You'll want to strike up your first conversation with the least intimidating person there.

Lastly, be sure to bring sunblock, a pair of dark sunglasses and a book. The sun block is for safety reasons, the dark sunglasses are so you can check out other people (because you know you're going to) and the book is to cover your nether regions when you realize you're naked.

(3) Senior's Club

WHERE YOU CAN BURP, FALL ASLEEP AND PASS GAS—AND NO ONE WILL EVEN NOTICE.

This is a no-brainer—join a senior's club. You get discounts on everything. You will meet lots of other people your age and there's always something to do there.

Here's what you can expect:

- Everyone that still has hair will have gray hair.

- Everyone will speak loudly because they forgot their hearing aids at home.

- Those that still drive will always be late because they still drive.

- Walkers will be strewn all around the place.

- If music is playing, it will be a mix of Sinatra and Bennett with a little Presley thrown in for the rebels.

- There will usually be a lineup for the bathroom so be sure to go at home.

- If you're still in good shape you'll automatically be the go-to person for everything that involves getting out of your seat.

- You will play a lot of card games, so brush up on your bridge and euchre.

- There will always be someone talking about his or her hip replacement.

- There will always be someone discussing toilet habits and what keeps them regular.

Everyone there will be retired... which brings us back to you. Join a seniors club.

If you think you're too young to actually join the seniors club, try volunteering there then. There is probably a lot you could do to help, and by the time you decide you're old enough, you'll already have friends there.

(4) Health Club

NOT TO BE CONFUSED WITH A FITNESS CLUB, WHERE PEOPLE GET IN SHAPE.

Health clubs are a lot of fun as long as you go with the intention of pampering yourself.

First of all, don't go near the actual gym, that's for those losers who still care about how they look.

You're way past that. Head straight to the hot tub. It's here that you will meet the real hard-core health club users. They'll be all shriveled up because they've been in the hot tub for two hours and will appreciate a new face. If the water stops bubbling, don't look down at the bottom, you don't want to know what may have settled down there.

Check out the masseuses next (the people that rub you). Look for one who is older and tired looking. You don't want someone who's too energetic and wants to chat. There's a good chance that you'll become so relaxed as they rub your lower back that you might let one rip. No worries, they're used to it. Don't be embarrassed, but you might want to double their tip.

Finally, head for the juice bar, they call it that for the gym users. But don't worry, when they see you coming it becomes the bar.

(5)   P o l a r   B e a r   C l u b

WHERE MEN ARE MEN.

Few things are as exhilarating as jumping into ice cold water in the dead of winter. It's generally done as a group, that way no one thinks you're just a rogue lunatic.

Basically, you all run into the water, dunk yourself, and then run back out again.

Now, of course you have to live somewhere where the average winter temperature is below freezing. No one is going to be too impressed if you jump into the pool at the Hawaii Hilton just because the pool heater is broken.

I'm not sure where this tradition started, but I'm thinking the Russians had something to do with it. It seems like kind of a macho thing that they would do.

Chances are there's a Polar Bear Club near you. I'm pretty sure actual polar bears would not be impressed with this. However, if you came up with a salmon in your mouth, now that's another story.

There's no special technique or equipment needed, but I'd make a mental note of where the guy with the defibrillator is hanging out just in case.

Be prepared if you're elderly, organizers might question your sanity. Bring a note from whoever told you to go jump in the lake.

(6) Online Dating Club

WHERE EVERYONE YOU MEET IS SEXY YOUNG AND SUCCESSFUL... UNTIL YOU MEET THEM IN PERSON.

This retirement choice comes with a warning.

First of all, don't do this if you're still married. That's probably obvious, but it has to be said.

The second thing you should know is that the online world is full of nutbars and absolute whackos. Some will be ex-cons, others will be mental health patients and most will lie about everything about themselves.

Okay, so now that we've set the stage, how do you get an online date?

First of all, find a picture of you that was taken 20 years ago. It's okay, everyone does that.

Next, say lots of cutesy things that make you seem adorable. You like puppies and long walks on the beach and romantic comedies. That kind of stuff.

List your habits as philanthropy and real estate. This will attract the wrong types of people, but you're not going to go out with them anyway. You just want to mess with their heads a bit.

The last thing you need to do is select someone and then set up a public place to meet. A burger joint is good, be sure to split the bill.

(7) Golf Club

IT'S CALLED GOLF BECAUSE ALL THE OTHER 4-LETTER WORDS WERE TAKEN.

If you've never golfed before, everyone will be encouraging and applaud your efforts. That is, until they're stuck behind you on the course and then their attitudes will change.

Spend the first 2 years on the driving range and putting practice greens. You can't do much damage there and you will look the part until you take a real swing at a ball.

If you want to look like you know what you're doing, hang around the bar (often called the 19th hole) and just join in on the stories.

Nobody there really remembers anything about their game, but they think they do.

They will go into great detail about that 8-foot putt on the 3rd hole, or the approach shot on the 16th. Notice these people are never actually sitting with the rest of their foursome. They all manage to spread themselves around the room telling their own version of the days play.

Just memorize a few jokes, buy the odd round of drinks, dress funny and you'll fit in at just about any golf club.

(8) Choir or Barbershop Chorus

WHERE NO MATTER HOW BAD YOU SING YOU WILL BE DROWNED OUT BY OTHER PEOPLE SINGING JUST AS BAD.

Ever had a hankering to sing Auld Lang Syne or Shine On Harvest Moon? Maybe you were meant to be in a choir or a barbershop chorus.

You probably already know someone in a singing group. These are the type of people that always have to be entertaining you whether you want them to or not.

You have your tenors, altos, sopranos, baritones and leads. The leads are usually the only ones who get to sing the parts of the song everyone recognizes, the rest are just backup singers.

I think a lot of people in choruses are tone deaf. They seem pretty happy though as long as they all start and finish the song at the same time.

If you're not really seriously considering this, be careful. They recruit retired people, in fact if you attend a performance you could be held hostage afterwards until you enlist.

Chapter 2:
Experiment a Little

(9) Smoke Some Pot

YOU'RE PROBABLY ALWAYS TALKING ABOUT YOUR JOINTS ANYWAY, NOW YOU CAN SMOKE ONE AND SAY IT'S FOR MEDICAL USE.

You might have done this as a much younger person, but if this is your first time be ready for a real head bender. You will start using language like *Dude!* or *Hey Man!* or *Let's Get Trippy!* You may also end up binge watching old Cheech and Chong movies.

Consider combining your new pot smoking hobby with your love of baking. You will find many marijuana recipes on the Internet. You may need to quench the munchies (food craving). The term pot belly isn't just a coincidence.

The world will seem all mellow and your cares will vanish, or at least until you need another ride on the wacky tobaccy train.

This opens up new possibilities for gift givers. Just when your kids have entirely run out of ideas for Christmas and birthday presents, now they can shop for bongs and roach clips.

You will discover many ingenious places to hide your stash so your grandkids won't accidentally discover it. Remembering where you put it is the hard part.

Expect to be a little self-conscious in the early stages; — after all, you grew up in a time when using Mary-Jane made you a communist.

(10) Husband/Wife Swapping

YOU MIGHT BE THINKING, WHO WOULD WANT MY HUSBAND, OR WHY WOULD I WANT SOMEONE ELSE'S PAIN IN THE ASS?

Well first of all that kind of attitude will get you nowhere. If you want to experiment with spouse swapping you must embrace the idea of acceptance and vulnerability. Open your mind and heart to.... Um! .... Who am I kidding? This is all about getting 'jiggy' with someone else's husband or wife. Just think, strangers one minute, swingers the next.

Swapper's should know what this is all about; you can't show up and pretend you didn't know what you signed up for. It's understood that your diddley parts are up for public display and attention.

This is a big step in a relationship and must be handled carefully. No one wants to think they're trading down, but then again how can everyone trade up? You'll never get that one figured out so your best bet is to just turn off the lights and feel your way around and oooh! and ahhh! a little.

(1 1) T r y N e w F o o d s

HOW TO TAKE YOUR GASTROINTESTINAL TRACK ON A WILD RIDE.

Let's face it, you've probably eaten the same 10 meals all your life. You had to think about what your kids would eat, what was in season at the store and what you could afford. Well those concerns are all behind you now, so grab your bib and the antacids, then head to the ethnic side of town.

Every culture has a 'weird things' they eat category, and you've probably said to yourself you'd never try any of those. It might be roasted toad on a stick, squid eyeballs, or bull testicles. People do eat them! In fact, they may be considered quite a delicacy in certain cultures. So, what's your excuse for not venturing out a little? Is it a weak stomach or a weak mind?

Here's what you should do. Grab a spouse or friend (might or might not be one in the same) and agree that you're both going to try something different. You'll be there to emotionally and physically support each other. Take them to a local Middle Eastern restaurant and order the fried crickets. Have them eat a large spoonful first. Now, run out of there... you're retired, not senile!

(12) Gambling in Vegas

WHERE BAD CHOICES WILL SOMEDAY MAKE GOOD STORIES.

Your kids won't be too cool with the idea of you gambling away their inheritance in Vegas, but hey that's their problem. This is how the whole thing will go down.

You start off playing the slot machines. They look simple enough and you can't screw up too badly.

You'll win a bit then lose a bit and eventually break even. This will raise your confidence. Now you hit the black jack table. After watching a few high rollers make it look easy, you take out your entire gambling allowance and buy chips. You will play 4 or 5 hands and win every time. It's so easy. Bravado will get the better of you and you prepare to bet your entire stash. You're dealt two face cards and you stay. Everything is going according to plan until the dealer deals herself an exact 21. #@&%

Remember gambling is only a problem if you're losing... and you will lose. But you'll have a story.

(13) Organize Wine Tours

I NEVER APPRECIATED GEOGRAPHY UNTIL I STARTED DRINKING WINE.

If you used to organize Pub Crawls when you were younger, then this will be a piece of cake.

Wine tours are the classier cousin and will attract a better quality of clientele. Because you are organizing things, you will be regarded as a wine connoisseur. This entitles you to swish, sniff, sip and then spit. That's never made a lot of sense to me.

If you like wine so much why would you spit it out? But that's what they do.

You might also want to look into a book and learn something about wine.

There's basically Red, Rosé and White, and they're categorized as dry or sweet.

Just for the record white wine is clear and dry wine is definitely wet. The people that made up these terms probably drank way too much wine.

There's no real magic to putting a tour together. Basically get a bunch of your wine appreciating friends together (nice way of saying winos), charter a bus and head to wine country.

At each winery you will get out of the bus and sample all their wines. You will continue to do this at each winery until you can no longer get back on the bus. At that point, you'll probably all sit around and sing 99 bottles of Merlot in the cellar, 99 bottles of Merlot, if one of these bottles... Well you probably know the rest.

(14) Go on Safari

ANIMALS LOVE IT WHEN YOU GO ON SAFARI; IT'S SORT OF LIKE A DRIVE-BY BUFFET FOR THEM. THE BEST PART IS THEY DON'T HAVE TO GO UP AND GET IN LINE; THE FOOD IS RIGHT THERE.

If you have a pair of knee length khaki shorts and a pith helmet, then you're good to go.

You will also need a safe-word in case a lion attacks. Just kidding, they'll attack anyway.

Ever seen a bunch of hippotamuses, hippopotams... ever seen more than one hippopotamus at a time? Well, if you see a pack of them, stay away. Apparently they are responsible for more deaths than any other animal in Africa. This has been happening ever since Walt Disney made them dance in those tutus in Fantasia.

There are other dangerous animals. Some are friendly looking and cute like monkeys, but don't fall for that.

If one comes up to you, that's the decoy monkey. It's a type of Serengeti switcheroo they've learned. While you're taking a picture of the decoy, another one is sneaking around behind you going through your purse. They get together afterwards and mock you in front all of the other animals.

You've probably heard of laughing hyenas? Well there's a reason they're laughing.

Chapter 3: Family & Around The House

(15) Downsize

YOU HAVE NO IDEA HOW MUCH JUNK YOU'VE COLLECTED UNTIL YOU DOWNSIZE.

You've lived in your castle for years and now it's time to give–up the throne. It won't be easy, but scaling down your home will save money and bring you closer together, literally.

Start with the garage. 6 shovels, 2 lawnmowers, 4 rakes and 3 wheelbarrows will make great yard sale stuff. Expect to be insulted by buyers. They will make ridiculously low offers, and some of them will be your neighbors.

Have this yard sale each week until you're down to one of everything in the house. You can make exceptions for dishes and allow yourself two of each.

List your home with a reliable agent; they exist... somewhere.

Next, start looking in the real-estate ads and remember you're downsizing. Note any homes that are half the size of home you're coming from. No one needs 4 bathrooms and a 3-car garage.

Watch for misleading listings.

- Newer roof — means newer than the neighbor's roof.

- Pool sized lot — means wading pool size

- Country aroma — means your downwind of a livestock farm

- 3 plus bedrooms — means two bedrooms and large closet

- Quiet neighborhood — means it's beside a cemetery

(16) Renovate Your Home

ALSO CALLED "HOW TO SPEND $125,000 WITHOUT LEAVING YOUR LIVING ROOM."

So, this one's a little expensive but it's potentially the most satisfying. You've lived in your home for years and put up with that crack in the ceiling or that cramped little bathroom, but not anymore.

You start by having an idea of what you want. Write it down and sketch it out.

Then you hire a contractor who will tell you none of your ideas will work.

They will walk around your house muttering to themselves and making their own notes. If you look closely into their eyes you will see pure evil. The pupils will be shaped like little dollar signs.

Whatever quote they give you, double it. However long they say it will take, triple it.

The day they show up to start the renovation they will bring lots of equipment and your excitement level will be at an all-time high. The foreman will then tell you the materials he ordered won't be delivered for 3 weeks.

Welcome to the world of home renovation.

(17) Spoil The Grandchildren

HERE'S YOUR CHANCE TO GET EVEN FOR ALL THE YEARS YOUR KIDS WERE A PAIN IN THE BUTT.

Buy your grandchildren a set of drums, a horn and video games. These are all part of the get even plan.

Are you asking yourself what these toys have in common? They're all safe for young children, they're all age appropriate and... they all make a lot of noise.

The best part is when it gets too noisy (and it will) you can just leave.

As you go out the door, do a little look back over your shoulder at your own kids. Give them a wink and one of those little pulling the trigger with a handgun type of gestures.

They might look a little confused at first but some day they will come to understand and do the same thing to their kids. It's a right-of-passage type of thing.

Of course you don't have to stop there, that's only half the effect.

Take your grandchildren out for as much candy as they want to cram down their little throats.... you know, the real high-energy stuff.

Then take them back to their home, drop them off and make a run for it.

(18) Jigsaw Puzzles

SOME ASSEMBLY REQUIRED.

If you have a high tolerance for frustration, maybe puzzles is your thing.

It also helps to have a creative mind so you can think of something to do with all those little pieces once you give up on the puzzle (think jewelry or a mixed media art piece).

You might be tempted at the store to buy the puzzle with the most pieces. After all it's more for your money right?

Well, although that may be true, you should start with something really easy or you could drive yourself crazy. Look for something that says from 2- 5 years. Hopefully it will take you a lot less time than that.

There are also other types of puzzles. Crossword puzzles come to mind. It helps to have a real analytical mind and know the meaning of words well.

If you think an armadillo is a military vehicle, you're

wrong; and if you think peccadillo is just a smaller military vehicle, you're even wronger.

(19) Get Fit

YOU HAVE TWO OPTIONS WHEN
YOU FEEL THE NEED TO
EXERCISE; DO AEROBICS OR SIT
ON THE COUCH AND WAIT FOR
THE FEELING TO PASS.

Joining a gym can be very good for your health and fitness.

The key is to go very early in the morning and get your workout in before your body realizes what you're doing.

Let's face it, no one likes to exercise but if you want to continue eating chips and gravy there's a price to be paid.

You can at least make it fun for yourself. Stand beside someone who's counting their reps out loud and count along with them but three numbers off.

Ask for someone to spot you while you tie up your shoes. And if you do the aerobics class, stand beside the instructor and face the group. These things won't get you thrown out because you're a senior and no one was expecting to see you in a gym anyway. If you're going to be a novelty you should embrace it.

(20) Nap

FINALLY SOMETHING YOU WERE BORN TO DO.

Remember when you were a little kid and you would have a nap?

You'd wake up and everyone would tell you what a good little boy or girl you had been for taking your nap. Well get over it, no one's going to praise you for taking a nap at your age.

It's a great pastime however and it's relatively easy to learn. I say learn because not everyone's born with the right mind set for napping. It's different than sleeping.

Napping involves 3 things. A place, a time and an 'I could care less' attitude.

There are different types of naps... you should practice them all:

- The kind you do, actually pretend to do, when people are talking about you and you want to listen.

- The kind you do when your spouse is watching something very boring on TV.

- The kind you do when someone wants you to do something else.

(21) Lose Some Weight

IF YOU GO TO THE BEACH AND
PEOPLE ARE FIGHTING OVER A
SPOT TO SIT IN THE SHADE YOUR
BODY CASTS, YOU MIGHT HAVE A
WEIGHT ISSUE.

Losing weight is no biggie; you just have to get your lips sewn together.

If that option doesn't appeal to you then start eating less.

No burgers, no candy, no life.

Yes, no life, no one will want to go out with you because someone on a diet becomes a prophet. You will lecture, roll eyes and tsk! tsk! tsk! your way to loneliness.

Here's a better option. Just eat lunch on days when you've had some exercise. This will really test your resolve. Now you have to decide how bad you want to eat... and how bad you do not want to exercise.

There are low calorie foods of course. Things like celery, lettuce and ice chips will get the weight off quickly, but you will lose the will to live.

Buy only products labeled DIET at the grocery store. Contrary to popular belief, DIET is not an acronym for Did I Eat That?

There's an alternative to all of this of course.

Get yourself some fat friends.

Weight is relative.

(22) Write Your Memoirs

YOU'VE PROBABLY BORED YOUR
FAMILY FOR YEARS VERBALLY,
NOW YOU CAN DO IT IN PRINT.
AND, WHEN YOU'RE LONG GONE,
YOU'RE STILL KIND OF THERE.

Ahh yes, the self-reflections and ramblings of an old person.

Who wouldn't want to read that?

Well you shouldn't care, after all this is your new hobby. But if you do it right, you can actually guilt people into reading it someday. Every time they write you something or send a card or say something sweet just remind them that it's going into your memoires.

There's no right or wrong way to write your memories. Just get down whatever pops into your head.

You know the best part of having memoirs is that when people start saying you're losing it, you can reread your memoires and look sharp as a tack.

Memoirs are just memories, you knew that right?

If you didn't, you probably shouldn't be trying to write any.

And if telling people you're writing your memoirs sounds a little pretentious, just say you've written a bunch of stuff you found interesting about yourself.

Yah, that's it, now you don't sound pretentious at all.

(23) Write Your Bucket List

A BUCKET LIST IS ALL THE THINGS YOU WANT TO DO BEFORE YOU 'KICK THE BUCKET.'

There are no rules per se, but you may be setting yourself up for failure if it includes massive amounts of money, a former more fit version of yourself or extreme sexual acts.

Bucket list items could include places to visit, exciting things to do and personal bests. PB's are things like total hotdogs devoured in one sitting or the most hours of consecutive TV watching.

If at least half of the things on your bucket list are illegal, it means you've got a good one going. An American female in her mid nineties was recently arrested for crossing off the last item on her bucket list. You'd probably be inclined to congratulate her until you find out she was arrested for triple homicide.

When you tell someone you're working on your bucket

list they will immediately start being nicer to you. They will assume the worst, that your days are numbered.

This actually might be a reason to milk the whole sympathy thing a bit. Announce your bucket list 5 years earlier then you expect to expire.

Chapter 4: Hobbies

(24) Antiquing

SOME MIGHT SAY WHEN YOU
WANT TO SEE SOMETHING OLD
JUST LOOK IN THE MIRROR, BUT
WE'VE GOT MORE COUTH THAN
THAT. PLUS YOU MIGHT OWN A
GUN.

All those things you grew up with that your parents discarded can be found in an antique store. The price tags will blow your mind and you'll walk around muttering something like, "I only paid $2.00 for that new and now they want $200.00."

You'll be cursing under your breath that Mom threw out all your comic books or Dad used your rookie year baseball card collection to light the coals for the Hibachi. The reason they're worth money now is because everyone got rid of them. So you're going to pay dearly.

Who would have thought that lace handkerchiefs and bedpans would be worth money? One you blew your nose in and the other, well... you know.

Pretty much every small town has a flea market, you should only be looking for antique stores.

It's much classier and you get to say that you're antiquing, plus you really want to be known as someone who collects antiques, not fleas.

(25) Fishing

ALL FISHERMEN ARE LIARS—
EXCEPT YOU AND ME... AND I'M
NOT SURE ABOUT YOU.

Be prepared to spend a lot of money on fishing as a hobby.

It starts out quite innocently, but eventually it will cost you $87,647 give or take a few bucks. The activity itself isn't inherently expensive, it's the upgrades in equipment that you'll spend money on.

It works something like this. You buy a basic fishing pole and hook. Cost: $23.00 and change.

Get some bait and 'Bob's Your Uncle, now you go fishing and catch your first fish! It's just a little minnow because that's all your hook was rated for. That makes you happy for a day, but now you want to catch a bass. For that you'll need a more expensive hook, rod and reel, plus... a small boat to go out further into the lake. Cost: $7,489.

You catch your first bass and are really excited. Now

you want to go after the big game trophy fish. That will require a much bigger upgrade to a larger boat. It will look good in the showroom, but of course to gct it to the lake you'll need a bigger trailer and truck to tow it with. Cost: $87,647.38... give or take a few bucks.

There it is... now you're hooked on fishing.

Just remember, if you've got worms you can fish... but you should also probably see your doctor about them.

(2 6) R V - i n g

IF THAT'S A NEW TERM FOR YOU, IT'S BASICALLY A BIG ASS BUS ALL PIMPED OUT INSIDE.

See the country from your living room on wheels. These are the ultimate status symbol and one heck of a lot of fun.

Recreational Vehicle owners have this road cult thing they do. You must salute each other when you pass on a highway. It's just their way of saying we are special.

An RV comes in various sizes and can be plugged in for electricity at night wherever you choose to pull over. If you've got grandchildren or another couple traveling with you, you can literally send them to their room if they become annoying. How cool is that?

You will get around 5 miles to the gallon so expect to spend a lot of money on gas.

Get an RV, you only live once and your days are counting down. Just think, you can drive down the road, hit a stoplight and hop in the back to get a sandwich.

If it's a long enough light you can even go the bathroom.

Once you are back in the captain's chair you're king of the road again.

(2 7) Woodworking

THE WORLD NEEDS MORE BIRDHOUSES, BE SURE TO DO YOUR PART.

If you like the smell of freshly cut wood and know the difference between a table saw and a seesaw, then woodworking could be your thing... and by the way, you can build a seesaw with a table-saw.

Woodworking is all about the tools, and you'll end up with lots of them because that will now become the default gift that everyone gets you.

All your friends will come over to see your collection. Many of the tools will still be in their boxes because you won't have a clue what to do with them.

On YouTube there are a lot of really detailed and impressive woodworking projects to view.

You will likely just end up building birdhouses, however, and pretty soon you will have given every one of your friends a birdhouse.

Woodworking really just involves two important steps.

Step one: count your fingers.

Step two: finish with the same number of fingers counted in step 1.

(28) Knitting

IF YOU'RE A REAL PARTIER YOU'RE GOING TO LOVE KNITTING... SAID NO ONE EVER.

Okay, so that was a little jab at knitting but it's the most quintessential stereotype for retirement there is.

If you like to sit around and talk while simultaneously doing something else, you should like knitting.

Personally I believe that's like saying to others, a conversation with you doesn't require my full attention so I'll do this while I pretend to listen to you.

Knitters love knitting humor. They like plays on words using knitting terms. Yarn and hooking come up a lot. Those knitters... they just leave me in stitches.

Knitting is going through a resurgence of sorts, younger people are taking it up and even males are known to knit.

No males I know, but I must have read it somewhere.

So to get started, all you need is that ball of string, two of those sticks and I guess a pattern of some sort.

Good luck, I hope that was helpful.

(29) Take Up Painting

WHY DID VAN GOGH BECOME A PAINTER? BECAUSE HE DIDN'T HAVE AN EAR FOR MUSIC... BA-DUM-PUM!

If you've ever been to a museum of art and seen a Picasso, Dali or Pollock you might find yourself inspired enough to take up painting.

After all, if this stuff can pass for art then how bad can you be? I hope I didn't just offend any art connoisseurs. Oh who am I kidding, I hope I just offended every art connoisseur.

Taking a class might help, plus you'll meet other artists. Most of them will be elderly ladies and males with goatees.

You can sit and listen to people talk about their favorite impressionist painters. To join in you could throw out some names like Renoir, Monet and Matisse. You'll sound like you know your stuff.

But, if you want to leave them talking about you after

you've gone, say your favorite paintings are Dogs Playing Poker, Elvis on Velvet and anything with those little numbers that you fill in with paint.

For the most part, all you need are the basics: a brush, canvas, paint and a bottle of wine.

The more wine you drink, the better your paintings will look to you.

(30) Read a Book

WHAT DO HEMMINGWAY,
SHAKESPEARE AND DICKENS
HAVE IN COMMON? WELL, IF YOU
DON'T KNOW, THEN IT'S
DEFINITELY TIME YOU READ A
BOOK.

Reading is a great past time, you can totally immerse yourself in another era or another culture.

The hours will fly by and you won't be able to put the book down. Books can even be read on your computer or listened to in your car these days.

Some people even read the last chapter of the book first to see if they're going to like the way the book ends. This is a very strange practice indeed. Don't be strange.

Some books have little popups or areas you can scratch and sniff. If you come across these, you're in the wrong section of the bookstore.

Paperbacks are good because you can take them with

you everywhere you go. Coffee table books look more impressive but everyone knows they're just full of pictures.

You start by deciding on a genre to read. Consider mysteries, science fiction or biographies of fascinating people.

By all means don't read romance books. You will inevitably end up looking at your spouse and wondering how you ended up with that.

(31) Photography

BEAUTY IS IN THE EYE OF THE BEHOLDER... ESPECIALLY WHEN YOU'RE TAKING A SELFIE.

Whoever invented the camera was a genius. It means we can take pictures of the kids, grandchildren and pets in seconds flat.

Today's cameras can upload pictures in minutes, meaning you can transfer pictures from your camera to your computer.

You can then store them away on the cloud, never to be found again.

Someone invented the name selfie. I suppose there has always been such a thing, but now you can literally take thousands of pictures of yourself.

You don't have to be a great photographer to take a picture, you just have to point and click.

If you want real professional pictures though, you

should attend a class. There you will learn about shutter speeds, development techniques, composition, lenses, lighting, tripods, filters and so much more.

And before you know it... you will ready to... move onto a different less complicated hobby.

(32) Sports

WHENEVER YOU FEEL LIKE SOME
TENNIS, GOLF, OR EVEN
FOOTBALL, DO YOURSELF A
FAVOR AND JUST TURN ON THE
TV.

Look, let's face it; you're no kid anymore. In fact you haven't been a kid for over 50 years or more, so get rid of any thoughts about recapturing moments of sporting glory.

If you do try, a bad back, pulled groin and sprained knee awaits you. You have to have a whole mind shift now when it comes to defining sports for your age group. The term sports can mean different things to different people, but generally it involves some type of activity and a score to go with it.

With that definition in mind, let's explore some sport alternatives.

- Find the cars keys is fun; you can use a timer.

- What did I come upstairs to get? Timer again.

- Where did I put my bowling ball? Again use a timer.

- Where's the remote? It's the timer thing again.

It appears most of your sports will involve measuring time... well, luckily you'll have lots of that on your hands, now that you're retired.

(3 3) B i r d W a t c h i n g

IF YOUR INTEREST IN BIRDS ONLY EXTENDS TO THE FRIED CHICKEN ON YOUR PLATE, THEN THIS IS PROBABLY NOT THE PASTIME FOR YOU.

If you like to stand around in the great outdoors staring at the sky, then this may be the perfect hobby for you.

There are no requirements other than the ability to point and yell bird!

Actually yelling bird is optional, but it brings a little excitement to this pastime, though it may not be that popular. If you haven't been told, bird watching can be a little boring. So don't go in with high expectations, it's akin to watching paint dry.

You can sit if you like while you watch, but the official position is standing. If you've ever been on safari, that same pair of khaki shorts and pith helmet will also make you look like a birdwatcher.

Binoculars are optional, but they come in handy when you're trying to distinguish a buzzard from a vulture. Haaa! That was a test, they happen to be the same bird but arc called different names depending on the country you come from.

See, that was a bit of bird watching humor. They're a fun bunch.

(34) Board Games

OR IS IT MORE LIKE BORED GAMES?

There's something about retired people and their board games.

Some games are very easy, you just roll the dice. Others, like Monopoly, you get to dominate people, have them pay you large sums of fake money, and eventually bankrupt them.

So what exactly is the attraction here? Unless you're playing on teams, most games don't involve any cooperation, in fact they usually pit one person against the other. In this day of dog eat dog, maybe a little cooperation is just what we need.

As retirees you have a lot of time on your hands, so you could get into strategy games like chess or risk. But if you're looking for the quick win then opt for checkers or cribbage.

All games can lead to good fights; usually anything involving everyone agreeing on an acceptable answer causes that. So, if you want to go home still friends, avoid these types of games.

Your best bet is games that involve answering trivia questions. Those make you look very smart, assuming you know a bunch of useless information.

But inevitably someone looks stupid and we all feel a little better about ourselves.... and isn't that what it's all about?

Chapter 5: Take a Risk

(35) Get a Dog

I WANTED A DOG AS A KID BUT MY PARENTS WOULD ONLY GET ME A CAT... SO I TAUGHT IT TO BARK.

If you've never had a dog, here is what you need to know ahead of time. They can cost you a ton of money in vet bills and you end up carrying their #@&% in a little bag.

There's no way to look cool while you're picking up poop, and now you have to carry it for the rest of your walk.

For all intents and purposes the dog owns you, he or she has got you trained to carry 'dootie in a bag.' Oh, and by the way, it may still be warm when you scoop it up. Sorry to be so graphic, but no sense being naive about these things.

There are some other things you should know.

Your dog will lick itself when you have company over, and it will not only sniff the butts of other dogs, but yours as well.

And getting it fixed or neutered is no guarantee it won't

hump your leg when it feels like it. At first when Fido gets frisky with your leg, it seems like a cute playful act, but you'll soon come to realize he now considers you his bitch.

So, if you're not ready for a dog—opt for a cat or goldfish.

(36) Go Back To School

IT'S GOOD TO BE EDUCATED, THAT WAY YOU CAN HAVE A LITTLE VARIETY WITH THE SUBJECTS YOU BORE PEOPLE WITH.

Classes will likely be free at local colleges so take full advantage of them.

You could study Roman architecture or economics, but do yourself a favor and take something less scholarly, like a cooking or a life drawing class.

In case you don't happen to know, life drawing is where you draw people naked... and just so you're absolutely clear, they are naked, not you.

It's standard procedure to draw the male genitalia as a blur; in fact you're really not even supposed to notice it. You will notice it of course because you'll be thinking about 'size' because it's human nature to compare.

Do not talk to them—the models—that's a no-no, and don't make eye contact, either. No offers of food or drinks should be made either.

If you find this kind of detailed drawing isn't your thing then draw little smiley faces all over your paper and tell the instructor you're actually just a voyeur who came to gawk.

Always remember you're a senior and can get away with these things.

(37) Start a New Business

WITH ALL THOSE YEARS OF EXPERIENCE JUST THINK OF THE SUCCESS YOU COULD HAVE WITH A LEMONADE STAND.

Some seniors have a tough time winding down after retirement. You've told people what to do for years and now no one is listening to you. Here are three ideas to try.

1. You could always be a Walmart greeter, but then you're just an employee again. Here's a better idea, gather up all your retired senior friends that might still want to return to work. Now, start a Walmart Greeters Training Company. Shazam! You're back in the thick of it, and you're the boss... business lunches, hirings, firings, yah baby!

2. Homemade something or others. It helps to add the word grandma or grandpa in front of it. Examples: Grandma's butter tarts or Grandpa's pickles.

3. Maybe you'd rather run an import-export business. That's just convincingly confusing enough to really impress

people.

(38) Become an Activist

I GOT SLIVERS AND TERMITES FROM HUGGING A TREE.

There are a lot of good causes, and every one of them deserves your consideration.

Most of the big ones already have a lot of celebrities helping them so they don't need you. Think about the more obscure causes that don't get any media attention, they're the ones you should be looking at. Ask yourself where the injustices are happening?

For instance, maybe you feel circus clowns are being overworked and underpaid. Just look at how they're all forced to share one little car and wear oversized shoes. Look into Clowns Without Cars That Need Fitted Shoes.

Maybe your feelings swing more in the direction of overworked orchestra conductors. They could really use your help. They're up there forced to be waving their arms around like lunatics for hours. They know that you know they can't play any of those instruments, so their only purpose is starting everyone at the same time. People are laughing at them and they know it. That's why they can't bring themselves to turn around.

Look into: Orchestra Conductors With Arthritic Shoulders.

(3 9) G e t a S e x C h a n g e

IF YOU'VE BEEN THINKING ABOUT BATTING FOR THE OTHER TEAM, THIS MAY BE YOUR THING.

This is definitely a game changer so make sure you're fully committed to the idea before going through with this. It's not something you do because you lost a bet or you called tails when it was heads.

You are going to lose something or gain something in this surgical transaction. It will also take a while to get use to your new parts, so break them in slowly. Head out to the local mall beforehand because you're going to need a new wardrobe immediately.

If both you and your spouse go for a sex change at the same time, expect it to be a big transition for all your friends. They've been used to calling you Bob and Betty for all these years, and suddenly now you're Betty and Bob.

This is one of those things that if you're going to do it, you might want to wait until you're away for a long holiday. It's not the kind of thing you do on a Friday and then show up for family dinner on Sunday.

(4 0)   T r a v e l

"WHEN PREPARING TO TRAVEL, LAY OUT ALL YOUR CLOTHES AND ALL YOUR MONEY. THEN, TAKE HALF YOUR CLOTHES AND TWICE THE MONEY." - UNKNOWN

The first thing you have to decide of course is where you're going to travel to.

Somewhere warm is probably best, and no one wants to see a senior with a runny nose.

Going somewhere with a foreign language means you're going to struggle a bit when it comes to simple requests or statements that you want to make. Google has a website that shows you how to swear in 80 languages.

Knowing these phrases in the language of your destination should get you through the trip.

Learn to say:

- How much? That's too much.

- Where's the bathroom? Why do I have to buy something to use the bathroom?

You also don't want to look like a tourist or you become an easy mark for peddlers and pickpockets.

These don'ts will help.

- Don't carry a wallet. Carry a money belt instead. Thieves have probably never thought of that.

- Don't carry a map and point at street signs.

- Don't pull out a handful of money and tell someone to just take what you owe him or her.

- Don't wear a Hawaiian shirt even if you're visiting Hawaii.

Chapter 6: Learn, Learn, Learn

(41) New Language

DID YOU KNOW THAT 'I DO' IS THE LONGEST SENTENCE IN ANY LANGUAGE?

Learning a new language can be fun and it's good for your mental faculties as well.

Do you know there are over 7000 recognized languages spoken around the world?

Of course, you didn't know that, I got it off Wikipedia and if it's on the computer it must be true, right. But most people know only one, so this is your chance to be a senior with bragging rights.

I also read that scientists say even learning body language is good for your mind. You should practice it 2 -3 hours every day. Do it in front of a mirror to start. Then when you feel you've mastered it, walk up to strangers and start a body language conversation.

Okay, I made that up, it's fun to trick you old people.

You can learn languages online, through emersion, or in a classroom. Emersion is where you just show up on someone's doorstep in a foreign country and move in. You will quickly learn many foreign words, most meaning 'get out of here.'

But seriously though, I would learn French. It sounds very cool to order your meal in a restaurant, a French restaurant that is. You can also just sort of mumble a lot and sound like you're speaking French.

(42) Volunteering

WHEN YOU DON'T CARE ABOUT MONEY AND YOUR SPOUSE WANTS TO GET RID OF YOU MORE OFTEN.

Being a volunteer is one of the most selfless things you can do.

Hospitals need volunteers, old age homes need volunteers, and churches need volunteers.

Volunteering for any of those places will get you a pass straight into heaven.

Of course there is also a downside to volunteering. People will think you work there and feel they have every right to bitch and gripe at you. It comes with the territory, so be prepared.

If you've been used to being paid for everything you've ever done, this may be another contentious area for you. Think of it as building up the credit for your next life (if you believe in that sort of thing).

Volunteering may determine whether you come back as the ant or the elephant, a pauper or politician.

Oh man, no one should have to come back as a politician.

Did you know that the biggest volunteer sector in our society comes from criminals? Everyone knows that crime doesn't pay—'ba-dum-pump!'

(4 3)   Y o g a

THE ART OF BENDING, BREATHING, MEDITATING AND FARTING IN A GROUP.

People that do yoga like to tell everyone they do yoga.

They'll somehow manage to work the word yoga into every sentence. They will tell you about the best yoga mat and the best yoga positions and the best yoga studio. I'll bet you're already tired of hearing the word yoga. Don't become a yoga snob.

On the flipside however, it is pretty good for you. You learn new phrases like downward dog, and you can avoid buying a lot of expensive fitness equipment.

At your age avoid anything called 'hot yoga.' That's where you're in a very hot room while doing your class. People pay extra for those sessions, but it's a big scam. Hot yoga was invented so studios didn't have to pay for air conditioning.

Your first class will go something like this; you'll lie on

the floor and just inhale and exhale for a couple of minutes. You will be thinking of how great it is, and you'll be tempted to have a nap.

Then out of nowhere, you'll suddenly um, 'let one rip,' then spend the next minute trying not to make eye contact with anyone, pretending it wasn't you.

Just when you think it's clear, the instructor will look right at you and say, "It's okay, you should let it out."

At this point you are finished with yoga and will never return.

(44) Dancing

YOU THINK YOU'RE DANCING LIKE FRED ASTAIRE, BUT YOU'RE REALLY JUST FRED FLINTSTONE.

Dancing with a partner is great exercise—unless you're just holding each other up.

Years ago they had footprints on the floor so you knew where to place your feet. Now everything you do seems to be subject to judging. Simon Cowell aside, don't ever let anyone tell you how to dance, especially those people from TV.

The key is to feel the rhythm, it should pulse right through your bones and then you just move with the pulses. I could charge you for that dance lesson worthy tip, but we'll let it go this time.

Dances have funny names like the monkey, the snake and the foxtrot. You might think we learned to dance from animals, but we're actually born with the instinct to move to a beat.

Maybe people have told you that you move like a well-oiled machine. That's not a bad compliment, but if they tell you, you smell like a well-oiled machine, that's another matter.

Dance is great exercise, so dance till your pants fall off.

(45) Get Musical

IF YOU CAN STILL BLOW, PLUCK
OR KEEP A BEAT, THEN YOU CAN
PROBABLY PLAY AN INSTRUMENT.

As you consider your choice of instrument, consider that some are held and are heavy... like a tuba. Others are small and easy to take anywhere... like a flute. And still others you can play while you sit in a chair... like a cello. Learning to read music is optional, just about any sound you make will be met with polite applause. People do that for seniors.

You may also want to consider the 'cool' factor. Guitar players are rock gods. Even if they're bad and don't know what they are doing, they can make a lot of noise. Other more refined sounds come from classical music, and distinguish the listener or player as more of a connoisseur, possibly a virtuoso. If that sounds like you, then a violin may be more to your liking. Other seniors might tease you a little, but you can always hit them with that little bow thingy it comes with.

Musicians used to have cool names like YoYo or Dizzy or Satchmo. You could bring back that trend. Think about your most prominent feature or something else that captures the essence of who you are. Like maybe Wheezy or Shaky, or maybe Squinty.

(46) Gourmet Cooking

OR WHAT YOU CALL IT WHEN YOU CAN'T FOLLOW A RECIPE.

This is one of the few retirement pastimes where you can directly measure the enjoyment you're getting out of it by stepping on the scale.

Any good cook is overweight, and I don't mean that in a mean way, it's just a statement of fact. Don't trust one who isn't. Maybe when people see you they are saying, under their breath, he must be a good cook; look at the size of him (or her).

Gourmet is a pretentious word that comes from the French, meaning 'good palate.' Calling yourself a 'good palate cook' would just confuse people, so I guess gourmet is okay.

You can learn a lot from watching cooking shows on TV. Be careful of any recipes that involve adding wine. The tendency will be to add more because more is always better, right? But you may end up with very tipsy dinner guests this way. Or not.

Lastly, to look the part you want to get yourself one of those tall white hats. They don't really do anything special for your gourmet cooking, but they're funny looking and retirement is all about having fun isn't it?

(4 7) T e c h n o l o g y

IF THE ROTARY PHONE WAS THE LAST TECHNOLOGY YOU MASTERED, IT MAY BE TIME TO STEP UP YOUR GAME.

Retirement is a great time to learn how to use all those gifts you've been given over the years that required some understanding of technology.

Don't bother with the eight-track or the Commodore computer, they don't offer tech support anymore. I suppose you could finally learn how to program the VCR but they've pretty much disappeared too.

Whatever your current level of understanding of technology is, there is a YouTube video that will set you straight. Hmm! Come to think of it, that might be another tech challenge for you. If you have grandchildren, this might be your best bet, learn from them... and the younger they are, the better.

Sit in front of that thing that spins around above their crib. It's called a 'mobile' and all you have to do is just wind it up or replace the batteries. If you spend approximately 45 minutes at a time studying that mobile, it will make you very sleepy.

Embrace the nap, you've earned it, and after all... learning technology is very tiring.

(4 8) S h u f f l e b o a r d

IT'S ALL FUN AND GAMES UNTIL SHUFFLEBOARD STARTS.

If there was ever an activity made for older people that just shuffle along through life.... well do I even need to finish the sentence?

Shuffleboard is a great retirement activity. You push a round disc with a disc pusher thingy, and score points when it lands on the target at the far end of the court.

You might have to knock someone else's disc out of the way in the process, but that's it. No heavy breathing, no sweating, just work on your tan and enjoy life.

You will find shuffleboard courts at most senior centers and maybe some parks, but many peoples first exposure to it is on a cruise ship.

That's a good place to learn, just don't slip if you're playing on the poop deck.

Chapter 7: Prepare for the Future

(49) Old Age Homes

OLD IS RELATIVE, JUST HANG OUT WITH SOMEONE OLDER THAN YOU.

You threatened to put your parents in one for years, and now your kids are hinting at the same thing for you someday.

Just remind them that it's not too late to change your will, and that you spent a lot of years changing their diapers. Now they will be able to return the favor.

I suppose looking for your own old age home isn't a retirement hobby, but maybe it could be. Let's not get bogged down with technicalities.

I'd start by getting a map and drawing a large circle around an area that encompasses as many of your relatives and younger friends as possible.

Next, you want to look for a retirement home that's smack dab in the middle of that circle. Now, no one will have the excuse that it's too far to come and visit you.

Check out some homes in the area you've chosen and rate them for activities that you will enjoy, like Bingo, Find the Bedpan and various card games.

Eat a meal there. You don't want to be surprised someday when you check-in, only to find they don't serve any soft foods.

Lastly, just sit back and count your remaining days.

(5 0) Cemeteries

THE WAITING ROOM WHERE YOU SEE IF YOU'RE GOING TO BE HEADED UP OR DOWN.

You know you're going there someday, so maybe you want to have a say in where that's going to be.

Is a nice view important to you, do you care who your new neighbors will be, is shopping close by? These are the questions that you have to ask yourself... or not.

Of course, none of these things matter once you're 6 feet under, but you do at least want to have a cemetery that is well maintained.

Spend some time cutting the grass, weeding the plots and trimming the shrubs—all steps that will guarantee your cemetery won't be used in a horror movie.

Conclusions

DON'T GET OLD AND DON'T RETIRE

Well, seeing as how that's not an option—at least not forever—get the most out of life by just having fun.

Get up every morning, look in the mirror and just laugh. If you don't laugh, all that inside energy will eventually find its way out lower in the body. But that's okay, have a laugh over that, too.

The next chapter is up to you. You've reached an enviable part of your life and what to do now is limited only by your imagination.

I hope you have enjoyed these 50 Things To Do In Retirement.

Tell your friends about it, send it as a gift to anyone you know that's retired or approaching that milestone in their life. Who knows, maybe you'll run into each other one day doing # (10).

:)

OK, before you go do these 50 awesome things, did you enjoy the book?

If so, please write me a review on Amazon!

I'd really appreciate it.

It will really encourage me to write more books for you.

I look forward to reading your review.

Bye for now, and take care!

Berger McDonald